WILD RIDES

Trucks and Diggers

New York Press

An Hachette Company

First published in the United States by
New Forest Press, an imprint of Octopus Publishing Group Ltd

www.octopusbooks.usa.com

Copyright © Octopus Publishing Group Ltd 2012

Published by arrangement with Black Rabbit Books

PO Box 784, Mankato, MN 56002

Library of Congress Cataloging-in-Publication Data

Parrish, Margaret.
Trucks and Diggers / by Margaret Parrish.
    pages cm -- (Wild Rides)
Includes index.
Summary: "Features the biggest and strongest trucks, diggers, tractors, and
other big construction and farm machinery. Provides stats and facts on each
model of vehicle, including capacity and size"--Provided by publisher.
ISBN 978-1-84898-623-7 (hardcover, library bound)
1. Trucks--Juvenile literature. 2. Construction equipment--Juvenile
literature.
3. Agricultural machinery--Juvenile literature. I. Title.
TL230.15.M37 2013
629.225--dc23
2012006080

Printed and bound in the USA

15 14 13 12 1 2 3 4 5

Publisher: Tim Cook   Editor: Margaret Parrish   Designer: Steve West

Picture credits:
b=bottom; c=center; t=top; r=right; l=left
Ainscough Crane Hire: p.10-11, Alvey & Towers: p.4-5c, p.6-7c, p.24-25.
Caterpillar: p.18-19c. Construction Photo Library: p.19t. Corbis: p.8-9. JBC:
p.22-23. iStockphoto: cover, p.1. John Deere: p.28-29. Komatsu: p.12-13,
p.16-17. Letourneau Inc.: p.14-15c. Mack Trucks: p.8-9. Oshkosh: p.20-21,
p.26-27. Peterbilt: p.4-5.

Every effort has been made to trace the copyright holders, and we apologize
in advance for any unintentional omissions. We would be pleased to insert the
appropriate acknowledgments in any subsequent edition of this publication.

Contents

Peterbilt 379 Road Truck

Peterbilt is one of the most famous names in trucking. The company's Peterbilt 379 was its flagship truck from 1987 to 2007, when the model was retired. The last 1,000 379s made were called the Legacy Class 379.

DID YOU KNOW?

Many semi tractor-trailor trucks have a sleeping compartment at the back of the cab.

The massive engine sits in front of the driver, inside a long hood.

Always associated with quality, Peterbilt trucks are referred to as the Rolls-Royce of trucks.

The hood tips forward to allow easy access to the engine.

STATS & FACTS

LAUNCHED: 1987

ORIGIN: US

MAXIMUM POWER: 600 BHP

LENGTH: 20 FT (6 M)

WIDTH: 10 FT (3 M)

HEIGHT: 11 FT 6 IN (3.5 M)

MAXIMUM SPEED: 130 MPH (210 KM/H)

FUEL CAPACITY: 222 GALLONS (841 LITERS) X 2 TANKS

MAXIMUM LOAD: 27.5 TONS (25 METRIC TONS)

WEIGHT: 13 TONS (12 METRIC TONS)

WHEELBASE: 19 FT 6 IN (5.94 M)

Mercedes-Benz Actros

German manufacturer Mercedes-Benz makes the Actros cab-over truck. A cab-over is built with the driver's cab positioned above the engine. This design is used in countries where a truck's length is restricted.

DID YOU KNOW?

Actros trucks are used to transport everything from dairy products to race cars.

The 2012 Actros were revamped to offer almost every application needed for long-distance trucking. Redeveloped beds provide comfort when sleeping.

Wind can slow a truck down. The Actros has roof spoilers to limit its effect.

STATS & FACTS

LAUNCHED: 1996

ORIGIN: GERMANY

MAXIMUM POWER: 460 BHP

LENGTH: 59 FT (18 M)

WIDTH: 8 FT (2.44 M)

HEIGHT: 11 FT 6 IN (3.5 M)

MAXIMUM SPEED: 120 MPH (190 KM/H)

FUEL CAPACITY: 159 TO 205 GALLONS (600 TO 705 LITERS)

MAXIMUM LOAD: 32 TONS (29 METRIC TONS)

WEIGHT: 16.5 TONS (15 METRIC TONS)

WHEELBASE: 12 FT 9 IN (3.9 M)

Cab-over trucks link with semi-tractor trailers to carry goods. "Semis" have no front wheels. Instead, they rest on the Actros' rear axle.

Mack Road Train

Have you ever heard the saying "built like a Mack truck"? These trucks are tough. Two or three trailers are linked together for long-haul transportation. The largest of all the Mack models is called the Titan.

The massive engine is cooled by a huge radiator.

DID YOU KNOW?

"Road train" is a term used for the largest trucks in Australia. In the US, these are called doubles or triples.

Mack trucks are known for their bulldog hood ornaments. The most powerful Macks sport a gold bulldog on the hood.

LAUNCHED: 1977

ORIGIN: UNITED STATES

MAXIMUM POWER: 600 BHP

LENGTH: 174 FT (53 M)

WIDTH: 13 FT (4 M)

HEIGHT: 11 FT 6 IN (3.5 M)

MAXIMUM SPEED: 60 MPH (97 KM/H)

TURNING CIRCLE: UP TO 82 FT (25 M)

FUEL CAPACITY: 2 X 132 GALLON (500 LITER) AND 2 X 70 GALLON (265 LITER) TANKS

MAXIMUM LOAD: 132 TONS (120 METRIC TONS) ON THE HIGHWAY

WEIGHT: 15.5 TONS (14 METRIC TONS)

WHEELBASE: 17 FT 3 IN TO 20 FT (5.26 TO 6.15 M)

Large fuel tanks allow the truck to travel thousands of miles before refueling.

Liebherr LTM 1500 Crane

This Liebherr LTM 1500 is actually a crane on wheels. It can be driven from place to place. The arm (called the jib) extends like a telescope and can lift loads weighing as much as several cars!

DID YOU KNOW?

The largest cranes in the world can lift a whopping 880 tons (800 metric tons)—that's as much as six blue whales!

Large fuel tanks allow the truck to travel thousands of miles before refueling.

Cranes use lifting blocks to pick up weights. The larger the lifting block, the heavier the load it can hold.

An extra jib can be added to extend the crane's reach.

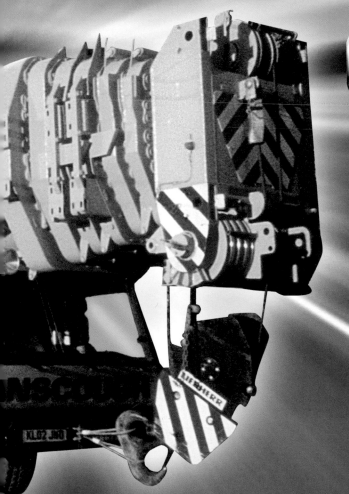

STATS & FACTS

LAUNCHED: 2002

ORIGIN: GERMANY

GROSS POWER: 598 BHP

CRANE ENGINE POWER: 326 BHP

LENGTH: 71 FT (21.6 M)

WIDTH: 10 FT (3 M)

HEIGHT: 11 FT 6 IN (4 M)

MAXIMUM LIFTING HEIGHT:
574 FT (175 M)

MAXIMUM SPEED: 50 MPH
(80 KM/H)

FUEL CAPACITY: 158.5 GALLONS
(600 LITERS)

MAXIMUM LOAD: 550 TONS
(500 METRIC TONS)

WEIGHT: 137 TONS
(125 METRIC TONS)

Haulpak 930E Dump Truck

Komatsu's Haulpak 930E Dump Truck is so big that it is not allowed to travel on roads or highways. It has to be taken apart and transported in pieces to a new site. Trucks like this are used in quarries and mines.

Sliding parts called pistons are used to tip the bucket up. The load then slides out.

DID YOU KNOW?

The driver has to climb a set of stairs to reach the cab!

The engine is heavier than the weight of the loads this dump truck carries. This keeps the truck from tipping over as the bucket lifts.

STATS & FACTS

LAUNCHED: 1996

ORIGIN: JAPAN

MAXIMUM POWER: 2,700 BHP

LENGTH: 50 FT (15.24 M)

WIDTH: 27 FT (8.23 M)

HEIGHT: 24 FT (7.32 M)

MAXIMUM SPEED: 40 MPH (65 KM/H)

TURNING CIRCLE: 98 FT (30 M)

FUEL CAPACITY: 1,200 GALLONS (4,542 LITERS)

MAXIMUM LOAD: 357 TONS (325 METRIC TONS)

WEIGHT: 192 TONS (174 METRIC TONS)

WEIGHT OF EACH TIRE: 5.2 TONS (4.7 METRIC TONS)

Letourneau L-2350 Wheel Loader

You could park a car in the bucket of LeTourneau's colossal L-2350 wheel loader. It holds the Guinness World Record for the biggest soil mover. Wheel loaders are used to shift mountains of dirt and rocks into the back of dump trucks.

A pickup, hoist, and dump takes about 25 seconds.

DID YOU KNOW?

Introduced in 2011, Generation 2 loaders are 50 percent more fuel efficient than the competition.

The L-2350 is a real monster. Each tire stands nearly 13 ft (4 m) tall. These are the largest mining tires made.

A wheel loader's weight is low down. This stops the machine from turning over on sloping ground.

STATS & FACTS

LAUNCHED: 2001

ORIGIN: US

MAXIMUM POWER: 2,300 BHP

LENGTH (BUCKET DOWN):
65 FT (19.71 M)

BUCKET WIDTH: 22 FT 3 IN (6.80 M)

HEIGHT (BUCKET RAISED):
43 FT 9 IN (13.33 M)

TURNING CIRCLE: 48 FT 3 IN (14.7 M)

GROUND CLEARANCE: 18 IN (.46 M)

DIGGING DEPTH: 6 IN (.15 M)

MAXIMUM SPEED: 10.5 MPH
(17 KM/H)

FUEL CAPACITY: 1,050 GALLONS
(3,975 LITERS)

BUCKET CAPACITY: 1,430 CUBIC FT
(40.52 CUBIC M)

MAXIMUM LOAD: 79.4 TONS
(72 METRIC TONS)

WEIGHT: 209 TONS
(190 METRIC TONS)

Komatsu D575A Super Dozer

If a heavy object needs a push, a bulldozer is the machine for the job. Komatsu's D575A Super Dozer is the largest bulldozer of them all. These giants work in mines and quarries around the world.

Tracks help the bulldozer ride over muddy, uneven ground. The tracks are made up of links, which form a flexible band.

The Super Dozer is twice as big as any other bulldozer on sale.

DID YOU KNOW?

This tractor crawler is available as a bulldozer/ripper or a dedicated bulldozer.

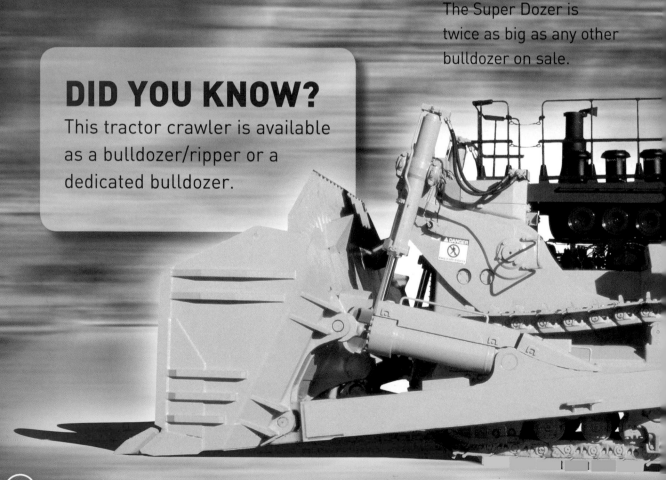

A Super Ripper attachment can tear up over 2,000 tons of dirt and rock every hour.

STATS & FACTS

LAUNCHED: 1991

ORIGIN: JAPAN

MAXIMUM POWER: 1,150 BHP

LENGTH: 49 FT 3 IN (15 M)

BLADE WIDTH: 24 FT 6 IN (7.5 M)

BLADE HEIGHT: 10 FT 8 IN (3.25 M)

NO. OF SHOES: 49 EACH SIDE

BLADE CAPACITY: 226½ CUBIC FT (69 CUBIC M)

MAXIMUM SPEED:
FORWARD: 7.5 MPH (12.1 KM/H);
REVERSE: 8.3 MPH (13.4 KM/H)

FUEL CAPACITY: 555 GALLONS (2,100 LITERS)

MAXIMUM LOAD: 31.4 TONS (28.5 METRIC TONS)

WEIGHT: 84.4 TONS (76.54 METRIC TONS)

Cat 385CL Excavator

Excavators are digging machines. Caterpillar produces everything from mini diggers to the giant 385CL shown here. A toothed bucket bites into the dirt, then scoops and tips the contents into a dump truck.

The excavator's arm has three parts. The boom links the machine's body to the dipper. At the end of the dipper is the bucket.

DID YOU KNOW?

The cheerful color of these diggers dates from 1931. "Highway yellow" made them stand out in traffic. It was also a response to the Great Depression, when many people were out of work.

The machine turns by stopping one of the tracks and continuing to move on the other.

STATS & FACTS

LAUNCHED: 1991

ORIGIN: US

MAXIMUM POWER: 428 BHP

LENGTH: 43 TO 47 FT (13.08 TO 14.30 M)

BODY WIDTH: 14 FT (4.30 M)

CAB HEIGHT: 12 FT 6 IN (3.80 M)

BUCKET CAPACITY: 81 TO 159 CUBIC FT (2.3 TO 4.5 CUBIC M)

MAXIMUM DIGGING DEPTH: 23 TO 35 FT (6.94 TO 10.58 M)

MAXIMUM SPEED: 4.4 MPH (7.1 KM/H)

FUEL CAPACITY: 251.5 GALLONS (990 LITERS)

MAXIMUM LOAD: 141 CUBIC FT (4 CUBIC M)

WEIGHT: 92 TONS (83.5 METRIC TONS)

Oshkosh S-Series Mixer Truck

This mighty machine is the Oshkosh S-series mixer truck. It carries sand, gravel, and cement. On the way to a construction site, water is added. The drum turns slowly to mix up concrete.

This cement mixer sends out concrete from the front. Its chute can be moved in any direction.

DID YOU KNOW?

The mixing system used in this machine is 2,000 years old. It was invented by a Greek scientist named Archimedes. It is called the Archimedes Screw.

After the load is emptied, the inside of the drum is flushed with water. Any cement left inside would set and ruin this expensive machine.

Blades in the drum turn one way to mix the concrete and the other way to push it out.

STATS & FACTS

LAUNCHED: 1999

ORIGIN: US

MAXIMUM POWER: 335 BHP

LENGTH: 40 FT (12.2 M)

CHUTE LENGTH: 22 FT (6.68 M)

CHUTE WIDTH: 13 FT (4 M)

CHUTE HEIGHT: 14 FT (4.27 M)

MAXIMUM SPEED: 50 MPH (80 KM/H)

WATER CAPACITY: 150 GALLONS (568 LITERS)

FUEL CAPACITY: 50 GALLONS (190 LITERS)

MAXIMUM LOAD: 353 CUBIC FT (10.05 CUBIC M)

WEIGHT: 61 TONS (55 METRIC TONS)

JCB Backhoe Loader

A backhoe loader digs trenches with its bucket. It then picks up the dirt with its shovel and moves it out of the way. This machine is useful in all kinds of construction work all over the world.

JCB buyers can customize their machines. They choose the size of the bucket and the length of the arm.

DID YOU KNOW?

Nearly half of all backhoe loaders sold are produced by JCB.

JCB has a team called the Dancing Diggers that performs stunts in a 30-minute show.

The operator swings the machine's arm around to work at the side of the loader.

STATS & FACTS

LAUNCHED: 1962

ORIGIN: UK

MAXIMUM POWER: 100 BHP

LENGTH: 18 FT 6 IN (5.62 M)

WIDTH: 7 FT 9 IN (2.35 M)

HEIGHT: 11 FT 9 IN (3.61 M)

SHOVEL WIDTH: 7 FT 9 IN (2.35 M)

MAXIMUM BACKHOE DIG DEPTH:
15 FT 3 IN (4.67 M)

MAXIMUM SPEED: 67 MPH (108 KM)

FUEL CAPACITY:
42 GALLONS (160 LITERS)

MAXIMUM LOAD:
39 CUBIC FT (1.1 CUBIC M)

WEIGHT: 8.25 TONS
(7.5 METRIC TONS)

Mercedes Tow Truck

When a truck breaks down, a tow truck takes it to be repaired. These gigantic trucks can haul two or three times their own weight.

Most tow trucks are equipped with floodlights because they often have to rescue vehicles at night.

DID YOU KNOW?

Some tow truck are equipped with winches powerful enough to pull a barge up onto the shore.

Tow trucks are built to the buyer's requirements. This one was used to rescue tanks.

When a tow truck arrives on the scene, a strong metal shelf slides under the vehicle to be towed. It connects to the front wheels and winches it up onto the body of the tow truck.

STATS & FACTS

LAUNCHED: 1985

ORIGIN: GERMANY

MAXIMUM POWER: 600 BHP

LENGTH: 39 FT 6 IN (12 M)

WIDTH: 8 FT (2.44 M)

HEIGHT: 16 FT 6 IN (5 M)

MAXIMUM SPEED:
60 MPH (97 KM/H)

FUEL CAPACITY:
132 GALLONS (500 LITERS)

MAXIMUM LOAD:
110 TONS (100 METRIC TONS)

WEIGHT: 22 TONS
(20 METRIC TONS)

Oshkosh Snow Blower

A blizzard can cover a road in minutes. This Oshkosh snow blower helps keep roads and highways open to traffic by breaking snowdrifts into loose powder and blowing the powder off the road.

DID YOU KNOW?

Attachments include sweepers, blowers, and plows.

This machine has two engines. One drives the machine through snow drifts. The other operates the blower, which shoots snow off the road.

The high-speed HB series snow trucks move 5,000 tons of snow per hour at speeds of up to 35 mph (55 km/h).

The vertical exhaust pipes are protected from damage by a heat shield.

STATS & FACTS

LAUNCHED: 1991

ORIGIN: US

DRIVE ENGINE POWER: 505 BHP

BLOWER ENGINE POWER: 650 BHP

LENGTH: 28 FT (8.52 M)

WIDTH: 6 FT (1.52 M)

HEIGHT: 11 FT 6 IN (3.5 M)

MAXIMUM SPEED: 45 MPH (73 KM/H)

FUEL CAPACITY: 2 X 125 GALLONS (473 LITERS)

WEIGHT: 22 TONS (20.4 METRIC TONS)

WHEELBASE: 11 FT 9 IN (3.6 M) TO 13 FT 9 IN (4.2 M)

John Deere 9750 Combine

In the 19th century, harvesting a small field took ten workers a whole day. More workers then had to collect the crop and thresh it to remove the grain. Today, a combine harvester does the job in an hour.

The grain is stored in a large tank behind the cab. The cut stalks (the straw) are left in neat rows behind the combine so they can be gathered later.

DID YOU KNOW?

When the tank is full, it can be emptied into the trailer of a waiting truck in a few minutes.

John Deere was a blacksmith, but in the 1830s he produced a highly successful steel plow. The company now produces equipment ranging from farm machinery to giant bulldozers.

The harvester cuts, collects, threshes, and winnows. Cutting blades are 20 feet (6 meters) wide.

STATS & FACTS

LAUNCHED: 1999

ORIGIN: US

MAXIMUM POWER: 325 BHP

LENGTH: 33 FT (10 M)

WIDTH: 20 FT (6 M)

HEIGHT: 16 FT 6 IN (5 M)

MAXIMUM SPEED: 20 MPH (32 KM/H)

FUEL CAPACITY: 210 GALLONS (795 LITERS)

MAXIMUM LOAD: 2,400 GALLONS (10,572 LITERS) OF GRAIN

WEIGHT: 22.5 TONS (20.4 METRIC TONS)

Glossary

ARM See boom.

AXLE The metal rod that joins a set of wheels.

BHP Brake horse power, the measure of an engine's power output.

BLOWER A machine for producing an artificial blast or current of air by pressure.

BOOM The back part of an excavator's arm, or a crane's long, extending arm.

BUCKET Scoop of an excavating machine.

CAB The part of a truck or digger that houses the driver and controls.

CAB-OVER A tractor unit in which the driver sits above the engine.

CHUTE A channel used to carry things downward.

CONVENTIONAL A tractor unit in which the engine is situated in front of the driver.

DIPPER The part of an excavator's arm between the boom and the bucket.

DRUM A metal container shaped like a barrel.

ENGINE The part of a vehicle where fuel is burned to create energy.

EXCAVATOR A machine that is used to dig large holes and trenches.

EXHAUST The pipe that carries waste gases away from an engine.

FLOODLIGHTS Powerful lights that are used to light up an area at night.

HOIST Part of a machine used for lifting.

HOOD The hinged metal covering over the engine.

JIB A crane's metal arm.

PAYLOAD The load a machine is paid to carry.

PLOW Machine used to turn dirt so that crops can be planted.

PISTON A metal tube that slides in and out of a larger metal tube.

RADIATOR A device through which water or other fluids flow to keep the engine cool.

SEMI TRACTOR-TRAILER A truck that is made of two parts. It has a front tractor unit and a rear semi-trailer.

SHOES Metal plates that are attached to each link of a crawler machine's tracks.

SHOVEL A scoop used to lift and throw loose material.

SPOILER A raised panel that limits the wind's ability to slow a truck down.

TANK A large container used to store fuel or harvested crops.

THRESH The method of separating grain from its stalk.

TIRE A rubber wheel covering filled with compressed air.

TRACKS Two flexible metal loops attached to some vehicles in place of wheels. They help a vehicle to grip on muddy, uneven ground.

TRACTOR UNIT Name for a tractor's cab, engine, and front wheels.

TRAILER A wheeled container pulled by a truck or tractor.

TREAD The grooves and ridges in a tire that help it to grip the road's surface.

WHEELBASE The distance between a tractor unit's front and rear axles.

WINCH A machine equipped with a heavy rope or chain to lift heavy objects.

WINNOW The process of separating grain from chaff (straw dust).

Index